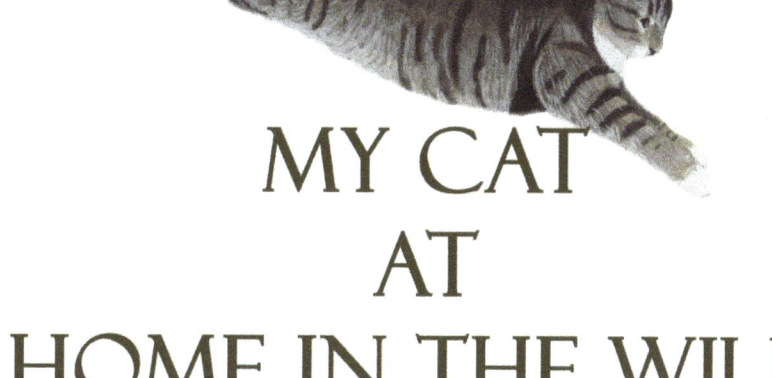

# MY CAT AT HOME IN THE WILD

by
Jennifer L. Rogala

Illustrated
by
Dwight D. Kirkland

"My Cat at Home in the Wild," by Jennifer L. Rogala. ISBN 978-1-58939-962-4.

Published 2007 by Virtualbookworm.com Publishing Inc., P.O. Box 9949, College Station, TX 77842, US. ©2007, Jennifer L. Rogala. All rights reserved. No part of this publication may be reproduced, stored in a retrieval system, or transmitted in any form or by any means, electronic, mechanical, recording or otherwise, without the prior written permission of Jennifer L. Rogala.

Printed in the United States of America.

For Nico and Gia who will, one day, grow to love cats.

I love my cat. She's a grey tabby with dark striped fur. The stripes over her eyes look like a crown. That's why I named her Kingsley.

Since I live in the city, Kingsley has to stay indoors. But sometimes I think she pretends that she lives in the forests, jungles or the grassy plains of the world.

At night, she runs up and down the hallway, like a mother lion hunting in the grassy plains.

Hidden behind the plants, she acts like a cheetah hiding in the tall grass.

When I'm taking a bath, she jumps in. If I forget to close the toilet seat cover, she jumps in there too. Kingsley likes to drink running water and has even learned how to turn on the faucet.

My cat loves our aquarium and is always putting her front paws and face against the glass. She's like a jaguar in the rain forest, swimming in a river looking for fish.

When she watches the room from the top of a tall bookcase, Kingsley looks like a leopard perched high on a tree branch.

She uses her scratching post to leave her scent and sharpen her claws. Tigers and pumas do this on trees.

Kingsley quickly jumps around the room, like a cougar leaping over rocky ground.

She climbs up the curtains, like a snow leopard climbing the icy mountains of Asia.

If a fly gets inside the house, she leaps high into the air trying to catch it, like a caracal leaping to catch a low-flying bird.

If she catches a mouse or bug that gets in the house, she brings it over to show me. She's trying to teach me how to hunt, like a mother cat would teach her cubs. I thank her very much for bringing me the prize, and when she's not looking, I put it back outside.

Lying very still, she hides in a box or a paper bag. She's like a jaguar in the rain forest, trying not to be seen. Sometimes, at night, all you can see are her eyes glowing in the dark.

Just like the wild cats, Kingsley only eats meat or fish. If she doesn't eat it all, she'll cover the rest with her blanket. She's saving it for later and doesn't want anyone else eating it. Tigers and pumas hide food under grass, leaves, and sticks.

When birds land on our windowsills no one else hears them but Kingsley. Cats can hear very well. Like the serval and the caracal, their ears can hear very soft noises.

Kingsley doesn't roar like some of the big cats do. She meows when she wants attention, purrs when she's happy, hisses when she's angry, and chatters when she sees a bird or squirrel outside.

When I'm vacuuming the rugs, she chases the hose, like a serval chasing a snake. I find many of her lost toys under the sofa when I'm cleaning.

Just like her large cousins in the wild, she sleeps most of the day. Sometimes, when I take a nap, she'll sleep on top of me, just like sleeping lion cubs snuggling with each other.

She leaves her scent on me by rubbing her face on my leg. Like the members of a lion pride, she's making me part of her family.

Sometimes, when I'm reading a book or newspaper, she sits right on top of what I'm reading. I guess there are times when Kingsley knows she's at home in the city and just wants love and attention. And I'm happy to give it to her.

I love my cat.

# Fun facts about the big cats in the wild...

Lions live in Africa. They like to live where it's hot and dry. Most cats live alone, but not lions. They live in groups called prides. The female lions do most of the hunting. You can hear the roar of a male lion five miles away.

Tigers live in the forests of India, Siberia, and Southeast Asia. They are the largest and most powerful of cats, and are strong swimmers. Male Siberian Tigers can weigh over six hundred pounds and be ten feet long. Most tigers have an orange coat with dark stripes. No two tigers' stripes are the same.

Leopards live in Africa and in parts of Asia. They like to live in forests, and where it's hot and dry. They are the largest cats that climb trees. Their spots help them blend with the grass and trees around them. This makes them hard to see. A black leopard is called a black panther.

Jaguars live in the rain forests of Central and South America. They are the largest cats found in the Americas. Jaguars have very strong jaws, and hunt on land and in the water. They are very strong swimmers and like to live near water. A black jaguar is also called a black panther.

Cheetahs live in Asia and Africa. They like to live where it's hot and dry. They are the fastest land animal on Earth and can run at speeds of up to seventy miles an hour. Cheetahs are the only cats that don't pull their claws back into their paws when they're not using them. This gives them a good grip and helps them run so fast. Most cats hunt at night, but the cheetah mostly hunts during the day.

Pumas live in Canada, the United States, and Central and South America. They are also known as cougars and mountain lions. Pumas have strong hind legs and are good rock climbers. They can leap up to forty feet.

Servals live in Africa. They like to live where it's hot and dry. Their large ears can hear very well. Servals have very long legs and can jump into the air ten feet high.

Caracals live in Africa and in Western Asia and India. They like to live where it's very dry. Their large pointed ears can hear very well. Like the serval, they can jump high into the air and catch low-flying birds.

www.ingramcontent.com/pod-product-compliance
Lightning Source LLC
Chambersburg PA
CBHW041438040426
42453CB00021B/2456